Layered and heartrending and transcendent, this is Ladin's best book yet. The speaker's nearly omnipresent fear—and acceptance—of the possibility of impending death are offset by her eagerness to speak, her expressions of love, and the poems' persistent music. And whether considering "the snake of time," the curving of eternity, or "plain old forever," these poems are chock-full of the myriad nouns of the world—which is to say the concrete feel and fabric of living: "I want to swallow the ocean of more, yes more."
—**Ellen Doré Watson**, author of *Dogged Hearts* and *pray me stay eager*

A Sapphic glance at the Pleiades; a Heraclitean thought on I-95; a siddur-derived "ritual for comforting someone afflicted by a nightmare"; a Woody Allenesque "death, shmeth"—these moments among many others blend into the improbably triumphant harmony of Joy Ladin's new collection. Woeful and ecstatic, earthy and ardent, *Fireworks in the Graveyard* enacts its title.
—**Rachel Hadas**, poet, critic, and author of *Questions in the Vestibule*

Today, "The world/grew wider, warmer, more dangerous,/more densely cross-referenced/with emptiness." Poet Joy Ladin again gets the temper of a complicated world—inner/outer—down on the page: "life may be all there is." Still, ". . . that tree over there [is] spinning light into sugar." Her poems rescue us from history as we read.
—**Hilda Raz**, author of *All Odd and Splendid*

The Zen admonition 'to live as if you were already dead' is suffused in every one of these watchful poems. Start anywhere. Or turn to "Balance," a masterful crystallization of what happens when meditation and lyric poetry become indistinguishable from one another.
—**Timothy Liu**, author of *Kingdom Come: A Fantasia*

Fireworks
in the
Graveyard

Fireworks in the Graveyard

Joy Ladin

Headmistress Press

ISBN-13: 978-0998761008
ISBN-10: 0998761001

Cover art © 2002 Nancy Macko. Thera 5, archival digital print,
24" X 24" Not to be used or reproduced without permission
of the artist. www.nancymacko.com

Cover & book design by Mary Meriam.

PUBLISHER
Headmistress Press
60 Shipview Lane
Sequim, WA 98382
Telephone: 917-428-8312
Email: headmistresspress@gmail.com
Website: headmistresspress.blogspot.com

for Liz, who watched them with me –
   Before you, even the sky was full of headstones
   Now, fountains of light

Contents

III. Finishing School

I. Fireworks in the Graveyard

While You Were Away

Spring fingered trees between nightly freezes.
Hawks built nests. Bombs
programmed to distinguish
tyranny from freedom
fell in a distant desert. The world
grew wider, warmer, more dangerous,
more densely cross-referenced
with emptiness. Another ocean
deepened between us. Love,
mine and yours and ours,
sank and surfaced and learned
to live on what it isn't.

Another Form of Love

We knew this would happen, that I would forget
how to talk to you, that you would forget
to want me to,

that our summers would split in two
as each of us remembered the pleasure
of walking around naked in upstairs apartments

where no one else is sweating, of feeling unknowable and unknown,
of time revolving under the private sky
of a world for one

sumptuously appointed with beaches and stones, grocery stores
            and bicycle pumps
and constellations of nameless others
who rise and set, dim or shine, with the charming irrelevance of stars.

Fireworks in the Graveyard

Ten headstones back, a family sprawls on blankets:
toddler sobs, sibling ahs, parents, stiff and a little chilly,
telling each other they're glad they've come,

feeling for what they've lost in the dark, wondering
what the kids – they're small – will remember when they're grown.
Explosions on the horizon. Fireflies and stars.

The dead have the night off, they don't celebrate with explosions.
Blue, red and white
streak the cheeks of a night

bursting with manifest destinies, yours and mine.
Rockets whistle past the graves,
rounded shoulder-rows of stone.

Mosquitos whine.
Are the explosions speeding up?
Is this the grand finale?

August

You haven't, you say, decided to leave me.

The sun is going down, the Pleiades
haven't showered yet, half-washed students
flaunt the misery of beautiful young bodies.

The moon fills like a basin with milk. Ears of corn
ripen toward forgiveness.
I'm starting to die, you're starting to live.

The snake of time
pulls its tail from its mouth
and tells the end to begin.

Afterward

After dinner, you browse, leafing through books with small white hands
that make me happy to have a body

even if it's dying
and you are frowning in distant sections

among the acid-free leaves of skyrocketing young authors
who make you feel envious and old,

the way I felt before my years
withered and fell away,

leaving me young and empty-handed,
dying quietly among others' poems,

the skin you touch from time to time
flushed like a leaf in autumn.

Aubade: After All

After all, I may not be dying, the dying I feel may only be
the dying part of me,
the part that's always dying.

My eyes stay shut,
I drowse for generations.
Finally, it's light.

Nocturnal insects still their lyres,
cars in driveways
doze like cattle, cattle doze in nearby barns,

souls in the neighborhood graveyard
savor the subtly differing chills
of dirt and grief and granite.

The sound of what survived the night
furrows the silence of what didn't,
waking me

to the not-so-complicated fact
that I may not be dying after all,
that life may be all there is.

Ephemera

Nancy L. Dole Books and Ephemera, Shelburne Falls, MA, July 5, 2011

I eat, I walk, I fall asleep in a straight-backed chair outside the ephemera
shop. How lucky I am

that my lungs still pump, my little rib-enfolded fist
still clenches with rage and swells with love

80 times a minute. My vitals are good, the sky blue,
clouds preen like swans in the shallow river.

The falls are close but quiet. Another elderly bookseller,
bent into a question mark, mutters to Nancy L. Dole

about rising rents and diminished interest.
How lucky that I'm still young

by comparison, strolling through the last few weeks of summer,
larks and swallows, hawks and buzzards,

turning from the clock-face of despair
toward the huge white face without fingers or digits

that tells the time of acceptance. A bit humid
but not too many insects, the perfect day

for ephemera to flourish, pains and joys,
fliers and candy wrappers, advertisements for miracle cures

no one's bought in generations.
The old bookseller's mind is wandering,

but he may be telling the truth
when he claims he got standing ovations

for the poems, a lifetime's,
he's burned.

Why I'm Not a Nature Poet

I wish I knew the name of that bird
I wish I knew the name

That bird keeps calling
I know it's a name

But I don't know the bird
Or the name it calls

Or if birds call names
Or whether the bird

Is calling or singing
Or whether that name

Is my name

Departure

The bus driver wedges Hegel's Phenomenology of the Spirit
between dashboard and window.

A girl chuckles. Lots of students on this route,
a crowd that gets the joke.

Hegel's dialectic ripens, synthesizing age and youth, eternity
and sweet September breeze.

Now that my life is almost over,
I wish I'd been better, more dialectical in my contradictions,

like that tree over there, spinning light into sugar,
or the girl exhaling dioxide as laughter, or the bus

filling with unlived lives
who have yet to learn

there is already here.

Corpus

I want to say goodbye to my body
before my body says goodbye to me.

We've never properly been introduced. I always call my body "body;"
my body never calls me at all.

On bad nights, I dream I'm being dragged inside it
but my body doesn't want to hold me,

isn't angry, isn't lonely,
friend or enemy, temple or ruin, shroud or sarcophogus.

My body slides like a bow across strings of time.
Gut and ribs and soul-post moan

through lips that are and aren't mine.
That's the closest my body comes

to letting me say goodbye.

I-95

We're heading south, sun in our eyes, stuck in traffic,
outdistanced by a dragonfly.
No one's moving, but everyone will arrive.

That's the nature of heaven and highways.
That's the nature of time.
The derrick hasn't stirred in days,

the waves of the historic river
stand frozen at the height of summer.
Pieces of heaven are tumbling toward us,

shards of sunlight
igniting yesterday's puddles.
We're moving now, rolling through space and time

at many lives per hour. There's a village up ahead, a marina, a bridge,
a flock of neatly nested condos, very exclusive, almost uninhabited,
one-, two- and three-bedroom souls, most with river view,

available for immediate occupation. The highway flows in both directions,
toward love and away. God, a helicopter overhead,
keeps an eye on everyone's speed, beating lazy blades.

Summering

1. The Subject Disappears

It's hard to make small talk
when the subject disappears. Excuse me:

have you seen my "I"?
Did it buy you drinks last night,

give you shivers,
stumble out at dawn, tail between its legs,

confuse its repetitive desolations
with the descending scale

of the owl that moaned in the distance?
Was it clever, patient, self-reflexive,

wedded to some dim, archetypal quest,
had it lost its sense

of beginnings and ends, did it stretch itself
toward opposite horizons, a tragic rainbow,

whose no could only mean yes?

2. Meadows

Spears and stems and pipes and blades, plumes, gone-to-seeds,
hays made, making and unmade,
succulent transsubstantiations,
wind-combed, bee-haunted, burrowed, barrowed,
lissome lawless legless legions
marching without moving, many
and no one.

3. Evening

Sunset flashes through tobacco barn slats,
fireflies flash in unmown grass.

Bowed black mass, a horse's neck.
In a pool of incandescence, a woman with shock-white hair

bends toward patio flags. Stars
thicken above her head.

4. Dusk Thickens

It's hard to move without scaring the rabbit
nibbling in the dusk,
fur blurring into grass.

The mountains settle into blank black mass,
cabbage heads rust
among drought cracks.

The kids are in, windows lit.
The rabbit drags thoughtful haunches
across the lawn. Dusk hovers

like a hawk. Time to nibble,
time – it won't be long –
to feed.

5. Sun Sets

The newly paved road is deliciously black, its oil ablaze
with plumes of sunset.
It's not my imagination:

the boy in the truck
is staring in my direction.
I must remind him of his mother.

The frogs have fallen silent. Summer
skips a beat, suddenly older, riper, slower,
rubbing against its own demise

like one thigh rubbing another.
A distant dog yelps. The first leaves,
like me, begin to yellow

near the top of a tree
that's otherwise alive and well,
struck by sinking sun.

Death

It's always summer now. Thunderstorms clatter past,
one leaf adds its green to another
until the trees turn black. A starved fox loiters in a narrow road

swallowed by woods
bristling with wings and webs, teeth, roots,
and many, many legs.

Nothing can stop growing, eating and being eaten,
the earth is furred with forest, loamed
with flesh and skeleton. The days

keep growing longer, night shrinks
to the paring of a fingernail, eternity beams down
on its favorite planet, the living planet of death.

II: How Much

Now and Then

When I get bored, I talk about life and death.
OK, mostly death, a word that sticks to my teeth like caramel.
I guess I'm bored.
The kippah'd man across the subway car
nods above a holy book that's losing its binding.
All books are holy, all bindings too, everything that's falling off,
and all the threads, giving way and holding.
I was the man in a kippah once, I scowled, I gave way, I held
to bindings I thought were holy.
When I got bored, I thought about life and death,
and if they would ever seem different enough
to tell which was which.
Now boredom is much more interesting.
I have someone to be bored with,
she likes to read and when she does
she looks like a slender silver fish suspended in sunlit water.
The city is full of people like me
who survived the winter
and people like me who didn't.
When life and death get bored,
we are what they whisper.

Sabbath

I didn't kill myself last night.

In Nepal, more buildings collapsed.
Helicopters hovered over isolated houses,
tallying the desperate and the dead.

Here it is flat and green and quiet.

Fewer blossoms on the apple
but down below, the lilac is still purple,
its petals still mix the sweetness of life

with memories of my mother.

Last night, I managed to walk around the corner.
Every step, a new sweet scent.
I couldn't sing to the Lord a new song

so I sang the old songs instead,

Be happy, heavens, rejoice, Earth
and *Come beloved and meet the bride, the Sabbath.*
The unforgiving and the unforgivable

walked behind me, holding hands.

Listen, the blossoming evening sang,
you have no reason not to die,
but you have reasons to live.

Amelioration of a Dream

The words in this poem were found in the Complete Artscroll Siddur's translation of "Amelioration of a Dream," a traditional Jewish ritual for comforting someone afflicted by a nightmare. The sentences are my own.

You have seen a good dream: merciful decrees, joyous laments,
transformations – seven – of evil into hair,

hair into lips, lips into clothing, clothing into dying, dying into salvation,
salvation into dancing, dancing into Heaven...

The dream is good, the dream was good, good will arrive in the dream
and fall like hair onto your lips.

Good will be your groans and your wine, your moon and your sun,
your sorrow and your fullness.

In this good, this very good, dream,
God's foot doesn't falter, God's help doesn't slumber,

you see the goodness of those who harm you,
the good that raises mountains,

the good that delights and establishes
a household where curses become a blessing

you make known the next morning
to three good friends to whom it isn't sacrilege to say

that goodness can be disturbing.
This is the good dream, the dream in which God undoes your lamentation

and says, for your sake – you are so frightened –
"You have seen a good dream."

Things With Feathers

"Hope" is the thing with feathers
Emily Dickinson

We hatch as you collect your letters,
fattening on bits of future

you always seem surprised
to find we have devoured;

when cornered become vicious; when trapped
gnaw off our limbs;

when systematically eradicated,
multiply within.

Maybe This Summer

Maybe this summer I will get better, my days grow longer,
my yellowed leaves green, my branches fill in.

Maybe this summer I'll be able to read again. My nightmares
will shake hands at dawn

and tuck in one another's organs, the world will spin
in only one direction,

the sailor demonstrating knots
with my intestines

will with a single jerk slip free and sail
toward someone else's misery,

and I will read again, paragraphs, pages, chapters.
Characters will commit charming adulteries in my head, scholars unroll

banners emblazoned with subtle truths
over ramparts of tessellated argument,

revelations will be published inside me in paperback.
God's ears will no longer be stuffed with cotton

because the closest I'll come to complaining
will be to say Amen.

Aubade: Walking Home After a Night in the Shelter

A convenience store clerk in a paper hat – white with a band of red –
sprawls on a box on the stoop, cheek to the humid breeze.

Squad car idles, a cop eyes the woman his mother's age
fixing him coffee with cream.

No hurry at this hour, nothing to avoid or achieve.
Even gravity is drowsy.

Time pearls apartment windows,
golden clouds pillow at the end of the street,

the pains in my chest, on my skin, in my seams,
burn like a ballet of paper lanterns.

A thread of river gleams.

Late Spring

Spring unbanking banks of snow, it won't be long
before you vanish
into leaves. How can I trust

what comes and goes?
You kiss, you warm, at night
you freeze, in the morning your sap

runs clear and sweet.
You tell me to go sugaring,
forage your forests, fill my pails,

relish the squish
of sodden earth
erasing the print of my feet.

The Water We Are

The stream of you
braids the stream of me. Braided,
we wash stones toward the sea.

The water we are wills itself thicker.
Whitens; ices over. We trade flow
for crystalline structure. Clarify

how thoroughly we've merged;
the strain
of flowing together.

Something's changed, some tilt
of earth toward sun
melts our grip on one another.

Unbraided, the water we are
abrades the forking bed
that breaks us,

you into you, me into me, separate streams
that share a source,
a destination, a sea.

Block Island

It takes the whole day to say "day."
Time tucks chocolates under our pillows, wheels wheel us –
wheels within wheels – uphill, down and up

to the lighthouse that's tiptoed for decades
toward eroding bluff. I rest on a bench
in a sea of green. You photograph the bay.

We've barely reached the end of "d,"
beginning of "day" and end of "the end," a phrase I hope
will take our lives to say.

Indian Takeout

We drink wine and feel shy.
Sauvignon pools in adjacent flutes. The glasses
kiss, we don't, I'm tired, you're getting sick.

Unromantic silence, one of love's favorite idioms,
just awkward enough
to be intimate. You tear

a poori pillow in half. Words
I neither swallow nor express
thick on my tongue like bread.

How Much

I could talk about being sick, but I always talk about being sick,
because I'm always sick, but today I'm sick
and happy, stuffed with fried artichoke, reggiano, gnocchi, and the glow
of knowing my name will be forgotten
when those who knew me are gone,
though of course I'll be remembered by God,
but will God remember the fennel salad and fried rice balls,
the candle on the table reflected in the wine
and the little flame when our fingers brush,
and how much I love the woman who loves me,
how much I love,
how much?

III: Finishing School

Finishing School

I'm learning to live by learning to die, hoping, this time,
to think my way from one to the other
without the drama
of leaving myself behind.

My self is growing,
my death is too,
a star in a sky
I can no longer say I've never seen.

Death sings from my rooftops,
serenades me day and night,
asking if I will learn to love this life
before I say goodbye.

It's time. My school, that is:
Time. I won't be graded
on a curve. Sigh.

Infancy

Once forever's lashes tickled my skin, voluptuous
but with zero definition.
I couldn't extract myself from the fullness of every second,
couldn't begin, couldn't end,

I wanted to love or hurt something,
I wanted to make a difference,
to stand apart, to be the thing,
the only thing, that mattered.

That was then. Now difference is all there is,
clumps of me and not-me.
Love must still be there,
but it feels like irritation,

and the oneness I couldn't stand – that seems like perfection.
That's irritating too,
longing for oneness I know I knew
but can't remember.

The universe is expanding, everyone knows that.
My hand slides between atoms, into the nothingness
the oneness I can't feel
must be holding together.

In the Hall of Minerals

Mineral sisters, who gave the fluoroscope permission
to flash your iridescence?

I know how it feels to have strangers ogle
my mounds and clefts, to be analyzed down to my atoms

to determine if I truly, elementally am
what my label says.

I hope I'm not getting too personal.
I, like you, became myself in darkness,

in carbon seams and basalt basements.
None of us is pure, we all have traces,

molecules we shouldn't, shattered lattices,
but we look so pretty when the light turns black

we make everyone wish their crusts would crack
and reveal what glitters within.

That's why they call us specimens.
Not because we're so very different.

Because difference is all there is.

Mid-Term

Have you ever loved? Answer yes or no.
Have you stuffed yourself into shapes and sizes, too big and too small,
have you papered your walls with pictures of yourself
loving and being loved,

have you papered your walls so thoroughly with you
that love seems eerily familiar, a repetitive frieze
of wishes and ghosts,
a story whispered under covers, beating like a pulse?

Yes or no:
Are you beating?
Do you have a pulse?
Are you ghost or whisper?

Wanting

Inside, I'm always blasting songs, tapping my feet,
learning to make my own fun
on the shrinking island of desire.
There's nothing left to want, and I still want it.

I want to be unique and have a lot in common,
to wear new boots over old sneakers,
I want tensions, energies, camouflaged agendas,
I want to try on nicknames as though they were pajamas,

to say "Call me Ape, call me Bull, call me Angst or Fuzzy."
I want to swallow the ocean of more, yes, more,
whose waves barely ripple
as it swallows my shrinking shores.

Not Unlike

I am not not, I am not un-, I am not unlike
a forgotten word
balanced on the tip of a tongue,

I do not dis-identify
with sparrows, snow patches, unpopped corn or unpresiding presidents,
I am not unsympathetic

to the melting of icecaps,
I neither confirm nor deny
the moral implications

of the disingenuous empiricism
from which I cannot detach myself
as I attempt to disentangle

filial assumptions from the flesh
of the son who turns away when I wave,
nor can I readily distinguish

the privileges of walking the earth,
earning, owing, giving and forgiving,
from the privilege of standing at the intersection

of subjectivity and subjection,
smiling at babies, singing psalms, confessing my racism,
telling a story that is not unlike my life

to a sky as distant as the ear
of the man my young son loved
when I was not unlike his father.

Centrifugality

I break apart like a family, my members

wandering off in different directions,
my reptilian nature from my conscience,
my stupidity from my intelligence.

I think of this as dying, though none of me is dead.
I'm frantic to bestow my innermost blessing,
but my innerness is tiptoeing toward the horizon

and my blessing has risen on its own two legs
and become the realization
that blessing is all there is.

My forehead opens like a window
I am climbing out
to scatter myself on the wind.

Plain Old Forever

Death, shmeth –
Been there, done that, conceived and aborted
innumerable futures
in a single breath.

Eternity curves and recedes
like a cheek I brush,
highlighting the contour of the bone
where being meets nothingness.

Even forever has a flavor, invisible and sweet, like a small ripe fruit.
Even nothingness creates a sensation,
like a pushup bra maximizing cleavage
between spirit and matter.

I was fine while I lasted, I'm fine
fading from lilac to black,
I'll be fine when I stop shopping and sweating
and slip into something more comfortable,

Earth soft as a moccasin,
plain old forever
sliding over my head
like a cotton dress.

Moths

Moths don't fear me any more. Settle at leisure
on sink and shade, row so slowly
the beat of their wings
stirs the hairs on my face.
Each day is shorter, each sun less eager.
It's the season of harvest, nuts and clusters,
mushroom-haunted dawns and dusks,
fattened calves, serious thoughts
about fixing roofs and growing older.
The light I longed for spirals closer,
overflowing every facet
of my compound eyes.

Unspeakable Truths

You look so familiar, and so strange, like old friends' faces lit from below
by a match flame. The smoke, I fear,

is coming from me. I hope you don't mind.
I hope you know – it's unspeakably true –

that I accept this burning
for a glimpse of you.

Balance

It's always evening somewhere, and now the evening is mine.
Summer's over, I'm moving on,
the shuddering pans of the scale subside.
I didn't fail, I was right on time,
the perfect balance is undisturbed
by the angst on either side.
I'm done with weighing and being weighed. Goodbye!
I soar like a balloon a child let fly.
The little void I held inside
opens into sky.

Window

The window opens, I mean my skin.
Now there's neither out nor in,
shadow nor substance nor point
to distinguishing planting from harvest,
happiness from pain,
traumatized from silly,
fountain from the rain.

Journey to the Center of the Earth

Earth is stuffed with graves. One of them is mine.
Here's where I should apologize
for fussing about a personal matter
and change the subject to the Holocaust, the Armenian genocide,
what Nineveh did to the Ten Lost Tribes,
Cain and Abel's archetypal tiff,
or how the Neanderthals died.
Why do we bother to kill one another
when Earth has room for us all inside?
My pulse is speeding up; why?
No one gets left behind.
There's room for every act of courage
and every single crime,
every evasion and shred of pride, celebrated sufferings and those we deny,
all are enfolded, held, petrified.
The tree outside my window
withering since the height of summer
has become the Tree of Life,
no fruit but plenty of branches
thick with pear-sized stars at night
I couldn't see when the tree and I
were still preoccupied
with stretching toward the sky.
Dying's not so bad, I say,
and even if I'm lying,
the truth is here, crowding the window
as soon as I lift the blinds:
the spangled wings of Earth and sky
furled around the tree
whose falling leaves
prove it's still alive.

Geese

The geese are leaving, so am I, our ragged formations
sink and soar, drawn along magnetic lines.
Life is the iron in our brains, death the wings
that beat to either side.
There are so many points on the compass now.
Every one is mine.

Hallelujah

I'm becoming what I've always been,
dust and silence, but also earth
and the hush of shifting soil,
silk splitting ears of corn, stalks snapping and sighing,
breezes, hurricanes, proposals of marriage,
hatchling turtles hissing on beaches, subatomic forces
linking arms in stochastic dances,
deeps calling unto deeps,
busy signals, outgrown terrors,
raindrops freezing into stars of snow,
the hallelujah of autumn angels
urging grass to grow.

About the Author

Joy Ladin is the author of seven previous books of poetry, including Lambda Literary Award finalists *Impersonation* and *Transmigration,* and Forward Fives award winner Coming to Life. Her memoir of gender transition, *Through the Door of Life,* was a 2012 National Jewish Book Award finalist. Her work has been recognized with a National Endowment of the Arts fellowship and a Fulbright Scholarship, among other honors. She holds the Gottesman Chair in English at Yeshiva University.

Acknowledgments

My thanks to the editors of the following publications, in which these poems first appeared:

Adrienne: "Another Form of Love" and "Plain Old Forever"

Atticus Review: "Moths"

Blast Furnace: "Geese" and "Hallelujah"

Bodies of Work: "Now and Then"

Cutbank: "The Water We Are"

Golden Walkman: "Aubade: After All"

Lavender Review: "How Much," "Balance" and "Not Unlike"

Mouse Tales: "Indian Take-Out"

Paper Nautilus: "Aubade: Walking Home After a Night in the Shelter"

Right Hand Pointing: "While You Were Away," "Departure" and "Centrifugality"

Rufous City Review: "Evening"

Southern Review: "Ephemera"

Storyscape: "Fireworks in the Graveyard" and "Death"

Sweet: "August" and "Afterward"

The Bloomsbury Anthology of Contemporary Jewish American Poetry: "Amelioration of a Dream"

Troubling the Line: An Anthology of Trans and Genderqueer Poetry: "The Subject Disappears"

Up the River: "Dusk Thickens"

Headmistress Press Books

Nuts in Nutland - Mary Meriam, Hannah Barrett
Lovely - Lesléa Newman
Teeth & Teeth - Robin Reagler
How Distant the City - Freesia McKee
Shopgirls - Marissa Higgins
Riddle - Diane Fortney
When She Woke She Was an Open Field - Hilary Brown
God With Us - Amy Lauren
A Crown of Violets - Renée Vivien tr. Samantha Pious
Fireworks in the Graveyard - Joy Ladin
Social Dance - Carolyn Boll
The Force of Gratitude - Janice Gould
Spine - Sarah Caulfield
Diatribe from the Library - Farrell Greenwald Brenner
Blind Girl Grunt - Constance Merritt
Acid and Tender - Jen Rouse
Beautiful Machinery - Wendy DeGroat
Odd Mercy - Gail Thomas
The Great Scissor Hunt - Jessica K. Hylton
A Bracelet of Honeybees - Lynn Strongin
Whirlwind @ Lesbos - Risa Denenberg
The Body's Alphabet - Ann Tweedy
First name Barbie last name Doll - Maureen Bocka
Heaven to Me - Abe Louise Young
Sticky - Carter Steinmann
Tiger Laughs When You Push - Ruth Lehrer
Night Ringing - Laura Foley
Paper Cranes - Dinah Dietrich
On Loving a Saudi Girl - Carina Yun
The Burn Poems - Lynn Strongin
I Carry My Mother - Lesléa Newman
Distant Music - Joan Annsfire
The Awful Suicidal Swans - Flower Conroy
Joy Street - Laura Foley
Chiaroscuro Kisses - G.L. Morrison
The Lillian Trilogy - Mary Meriam
Lady of the Moon - Amy Lowell, Lillian Faderman, Mary Meriam
Irresistible Sonnets - ed. Mary Meriam

Lavender Review - ed. Mary Meriam